a a social  an actor something from r to please the minister, decided to recite the Twenty-Third Psalm. With perfect diction, elocution and in delicate shades of tone, he repeated the psalm in a manner that caused the audience to reveal their enthusiastic praise and applause.

Afterward, the actor, in order to honor the minister, asked if he would recite something for them. The minister could not think of anything and decided, if it was okay with everyone present, to repeat the Twenty-Third Psalm. Quietly, prayerfully, he slowly began to speak out the psalm as it came to mind. At its end, those in attendance sat hushed.

Taking the preacher's hand in his, the actor said, "We both know the psalm, but it is clear to us all, that you know the Shepherd."

My prayer for you as you read this book is that you will not just know the Shepherd by name, but will know the Shepherd in your heart.

Roy Lessin

Psalm 23

Psalm 23

...verse by verse & thought by thought...

Roy Lessin

Kansas City

© 2020 Roy Lessin
ISBN 978-0-9983718-3-2

All rights reserved. No part of this publication may be reproduced, distributed, or transmitted in any form or by any means, including photocopying, recording, or other electronic or mechanical methods, without the prior written permission of the publisher, except in the case of brief quotations embodied in critical reviews and certain other non-commercial uses permitted by copyright law.

Churches and other non-commercial interests may reproduce portions of this book without the express written permission of the publisher, provided that the text does not exceed 500 words and that the text is not material quoted from another publisher. When reproducing text from this book, include the following credit line: "From *Psalm 23: Verse by Verse & Thought by Thought*, published by Art Set Apart, Inc. Used by permission."

Scripture quotations are taken from the Holy Bible, King James Version.

Edited by Kristin Morris.

Cover photo by Joe Lessin.
Cover design by Brent Morris.
Layout design by Kristin Morris.

Published by Art Set Apart, Inc.
PO Box 9064
Shawnee Mission, KS 66201-9064
www.setapartkc.com

Printed in the United States of America
First Printing 2010

Psalm 23

¹ The LORD is my Shepherd;
   I shall not want.

² He maketh me to lie down in
   green pastures: He leadeth me
   beside the still waters.

³ He restoreth my soul:
   He leadeth me in the
   paths of righteousness
   for His Name's sake.

⁴ Yea, though I walk through
   the valley of the shadow of death,
   I will fear no evil: for Thou art
   with me; Thy rod and Thy staff
   they comfort me.

⁵ Thou preparest a table before me
   in the presence of mine enemies:
   Thou anointest my head with oil;
   my cup runneth over.

⁶ Surely goodness and mercy
   shall follow me all the days
   of my life: and I will dwell in
   the house of the LORD forever.

Verse 1

> "The LORD is my Shepherd;
> I shall not want."
>
> PSALM 23:1

The Lord: Yahweh. The Eternal. Jehovah. I Am. The Self-Existent One. The God of forever and ever.

is: Not will be one day. Not someday. Not was a long time ago. Is now, at this very moment—as I draw each breath, as I take each step, as I face each circumstance of life.

my: Not just someone else's. Not just the pastor's. Not just the missionary's. Not just the people in the Bible. Personal God. My God. Knowing me intimately, watching me carefully, loving me fully.

Shepherd: Pastor. The One who tends, keeps, guards, guides. The Good Shepherd; The Great Shepherd; The Chief Shepherd. The One who leads. The One who feeds. Life giver. Care giver. Watching every moment; protecting in every situation; providing every need. Laying down His life. Giving His all. Seeking me. Carrying me. Holding me close.

I: His hand is on me. I am the apple of His eye. I am His beloved. I am His child. I am His possession. I belong to Him. I am in His hands. I am in His thoughts. I am on His heart.

shall not: Never! Not once! Not in any circumstance; not in any trial; not at any age. I am certain, sure, persuaded, unmistaken, absolutely confident of His "Yes" to me.

want: He is my supply. He is my provider. He is my provision. I shall not be given a stone instead of bread. I shall not come up empty, be destitute, find out that I have been forsaken. In Him, my Lord, my God, my Shepherd, my Pastor, I find no lack.

THOUGHT BY THOUGHT

Verse 2

"He maketh me
to lie down
in green pastures:
He leadeth me
beside the still waters."

PSALM 23:2

He: Not fate. Not "the gods." Not luck. Not self-help. Not philosophy. He alone! Creator God. Father, Son, Holy Spirit. Maker of all things. Keeper of all things. Ruler of all things in heaven, in earth, in my life.

maketh: Not wishful thinking, not pie-in-the-sky, but reality. He makes the way and gives the opportunity. He leads me to His prepared place. He makes it possible in every circumstance. He lets me; He insists upon it—I do not need to question or wonder what His will is in the matter.

me: Personal God! He understands my particular needs and knows where and how to look after me. His gaze is on me. His care is upon me. His love is over me.

to lie down: Legs folded, knees bent. No striving. No panic. No running about in haste or going around in circles. A time to stop, to kneel, to bend. Reclining—no "standing up" on the inside in protest or rebellion.

in: Not in imagination. Not in fantasy. Not in pretend or make believe. In truth. In my heart, in my soul, in my spirit. In Him—the Way, the Truth, the Life.

green pastures: His tender, caring place. Luscious. Satisfying. Nurturing. Sustaining. Refreshing. Delighting. Pastures free of dryness, emptiness, barrenness, hopelessness, despair, confusion, death.

He: Not governments. Not politicians. Not political parties. Not programs. Not schemes and the plans of men. He alone! Mighty God, ruler of the land and sea. Giver and sustainer of my life—my glory and the lifter of my head.

leadeth me: Not pushing. Not driving. Not far removed, but ever-present, ever-near. Out front. Taking the first steps, going before, making the pathway passable, possible, doable with footsteps of grace.

beside: Not looking at His provisions from a distance. Not far off. Not held at a distance. Not watching someone else enjoy His blessings while I am asked to take a step back, or step aside. Close. Near.

Placing me right where I need to be…
right where He is.

the still waters: Not babbling brooks,
not shooting rapids, but peaceful pools. No turmoil.
Not a place to rile up, but a place to calm down.
A still place, a quiet place, a restful place. To be as
still as He is, because He gives His peace. Here
I leave everything in His care and His keeping…
letting go so He can hold all. My heart is quiet,
my soul is still.

Verse 3

"He restoreth my soul:
He leadeth me in
the paths of righteousness
for His Name's sake."

PSALM 23:3

He: The God of all grace and tender mercies. The God of living waters. The God of healing rain. Great Physician—whose healing balm mends my wounds, soothes my pains, comforts my troubled heart. Redeemer. Friend. The One who always is calling the wanderer to return to Him. God of the welcoming voice, the gentle way, the reassuring touch.

restoreth: Not neglecting. Not ignoring. Not denying. Assuring me "He can" and "He will." Never turning His back or giving up. Lifting me when I am down; carrying me when I have fallen; refreshing me when I am stale; renewing me when I am weary; reviving me when I have grown cold; turning my head when I have become distracted; rescuing me when I am in danger; pulling me back when I am drifting away. Trimming my wick. Pruning my branches. Molding and shaping my clay within His masterful hands to conform me to His image. Making all things new.

my soul: Who I am in reality. My personality in all its complexity. My mind—thoughts and plans, what I think upon, what I dwell upon. My emotions—feelings, moods, highs and lows. My will—choices, decisions, what I determine to do, where I determine to go. My appetites. My longings. His grace causing me to think His thoughts, feel what He feels, choose what He chooses. Bringing within me the times of refreshing that come from the presence of the Lord.

He: Not astrology. Not philosophy. My God, My Guide, My Guardian. He, from whom are all things, by whom are all things, through whom are all things. He, in whom I live, and move, and have my being. Son of Righteousness. The One who never leaves me or forsakes me. The ever-present help in time of need. The only true time-traveler.

leadeth me: Not pointlessly. Not wrongfully. Not mischievously. Not aimlessly. Knowing what He is doing. Knowing where He is going. Knowing what is best. Showing the way, making the way, providing the way, being the way. Bestowing the blessings that make me rich; bringing the joys that make me full; imparting the strength that makes me able to follow His footsteps.

in the paths of righteousness: Not vanity. Not sin. Not selfishness. Making straight paths for my feet—not the path of self-effort, not the path of self-righteousness, not the path of dead works. A path of mercy. A path of faith. A path of rest. A path that keeps me from regrets. Freeing me from restlessness and anxiousness; from the hurts and disappointments of life; from the worries and fears that want to cast their shadow upon the course He has chosen for me to follow. Walking step by step on the highway of holiness. His righteousness. Right thinking. Right living. Right choices. Right attitudes. Right motives. A beautiful path. A peaceful path. A joy-filled path that leads me straight to His heart.

for His Name's sake: Not for my applause, recognition, or celebration. Not my light, but His glory. Not my reputation, but His honor. Not my cleverness, but His majesty. Holy One. Mighty One. Wondrous One. Awesome One. Amazing God. Name above all names. King above all kings. Lord above all lords. Transcendent. Immutable. Worthy to receive all the praise and thanks my heart can give.

Verse 4

"Yea, though I walk through the valley of the shadow of death, I will fear no evil: for Thou art with me; Thy rod and Thy staff they comfort me."

PSALM 23:4

Yea: "Yes" to You, Jesus. "Yes" to Your will, Your way, Your plan, Your purpose. "Yes" to what seems possible and impossible. "Yes" to what You have prepared, to where Your footsteps are going—through places unknown, to destinations unimagined, by pathways never taken before.

Though I walk: Not in panic, not in haste, not in perplexity. Walking, not running ahead. Walking, not dragging behind. Walking, not passive. Walking, not digging in my heels. Walking forwards, not backwards. Going at His pace. Planting my feet in His freshest footprints. Moving through. Not getting bogged down. Not getting stuck. Not standing in place and marking time. Pressing on.

Through the valley: Not always through the high places, not always through the mountain tops, not always through the grasslands, not always through the woodlands, not always through the bright and brilliant flowering fields and open skies of blue. Not the place where the journey ends, but where the journey takes on new depths and new meaning. The hidden place that presses me to His side, to His heartbeat, to His tender mercies.

of the shadow of death: Tears. Sorrow. Trials and testing. The place where seeds of desires and expectations fall into the ground. The place where I let go, surrender all, declare from the depths of my being, "Not my will, but Thine be done." The place where I embrace His cross, be made conformable to His death, where I partake of the fellowship of His sufferings. The place where resurrection life overtakes me, overshadows me, overwhelms me. The place where I feel His hand in mine—Firm. Sure. Mighty. Never letting go—taking me on to the place of abundance.

I will fear no evil: The enemy, a defeated foe. His works destroyed by the power of Christ. Jesus my victor. Conquering King. Captain of my soul. Holy Spirit—Spirit, not of fear, but of power, love, and a sound mind. Heavenly Father—the One whom I have sought with all my heart; the One Who hears and answers my prayer; the One Who consistently, faithfully, triumphantly, delivers me from all my fears.

for Thou art with me: There can be nothing sweeter, nearer, dearer, than this—"Thou," Creator God, lover of my soul—with me, near me, by me, for me, in me. Fullness of joy! Pleasures forevermore! Not playing hide-and-seek with my soul, my heart, or my very being. Ever present help in time of need.

Thy rod and Thy staff: The things You use to reach me, teach me, shape me, mold me, conform me, direct me, assure me, protect me. The rod of correction that never harms or is an instrument of abuse. The staff that pulls me close when I wander, that rescues me from the pit when I fall. Letting nothing slip by. Doing everything in love and for love's sake.

They comfort me: Not frustrates. Not bullies. Not stresses. Not "beat up." Not left in ruins. Not deserted. Not abandoned. Not devastated. Not destroyed. God of sweet consolation. God who wipes my tears. God who carries my burdens. God who knows me, cares for me, lifts me, holds me. Taking full responsibility for my life which I have yielded to Him.

Verse 5

"Thou preparest
a table before me
in the presence
of mine enemies:
Thou anointest
my head with oil;
my cup runneth over."

PSALM 23:5

THOUGHT BY THOUGHT

Thou: God of details. God who provides. God of Abraham. My God. Jehovah-Jireh. The One who sees, knows, cares.

preparest: Every place prepared before I arrive; every provision met before I am even aware of what I need. Not haphazard. Not unplanned. God ordered. God ordained. God maintained. God sustained. All things set in dazzling array, in its proper place, for its proper purpose, in its proper time. The plans of His heart being revealed to me.

a table: God's table. A daily table. A forever table. A table set by Him. His gathering place. His dining place. His banqueting place. Beautifully arranged. Abundantly filled. A place of feasting, of communion, of pleasures forevermore. A place where I can linger. A place to speak of His victories, to celebrate His joys, to learn of His ways, to share in the things that delight His heart and mine. A place where I can taste and see that the Lord is good.

before me: My special place. Reserved. Complete with my own nametag. The perfect spot. Seated right next to Him. Receiving my portion directly from His hand. Leaning my head against His breast. Knowing I belong. Knowing I am right where I need to be, right where I want to be, right where I was made to be—breaking bread at the family table.

in the presence of mine enemies: Not in la-la-land. Not in a make-believe world where difficulties, temptations, and the forces of evil do not exist. Being in His light while surrounded by darkness; feasting upon His truth though lies and deception lurk in the shadows; receiving His affirming love while voices of accusation and condemnation cry out to get my attention. Knowing He is for me even though the enemy comes against me. Certain that no foe can keep me out, shut me out, or cut me off from what He has prepared at His table. Knowing He is my portion. Certain He is enough.

Thou: Abba Father. The One who calls me His own. God of every invitation to be where He is. The One who says, "Come follow Me." "Come be with Me." "Come know Me." "Come sup with Me." The Host of all hosts, greeting me with welcome arms.

anointest my head with oil: Anointed by my King and High Priest. Anointed with the oil of gladness. Anointed with the anointment of

His fragrance. Equipped. Enabled. Empowered. Holy Oil— making my face to shine; causing my heart to sing; softening my hands to touch others. Refreshing my life, restoring my soul, renewing my spirit— protecting me from being sun-parched, keeping me from being weather beaten, shielding me from all that would crack, dry, deplete, blister. Fresh oil. Every flowing. Ever being poured out upon me.

my cup: Earthen cup. Heart-shaped. Cup of need. Cup of longing. Cup of thirsting after Him. Lifted up for filling. Lifted up to receive. Cup of trust, cup of faith. Cup of asking, cup of drinking. Cup of blessings, cup of everlasting joy.

runneth over: God of abundance! Not drip-drops. Not trickles. Not small portions. Not rations. Not squeezing out a little moisture from His promises. God of the pouring forth. God of the rivers of living water. God of the waterfalls of grace. God of the artesian well. God of the showers of blessing. God of the exceeding, abundantly above. God of the overflow. God of the more than I could ever ask or think. God of so much more. Allowing me to drink of everything pure, everything good, everything right, everything true, everything satisfying, everything that flows from His heart to mine.

Verse 6

"Surely goodness
and mercy
shall follow me
all the days of my life:
and I will dwell
in the house of
the LORD forever."

PSALM 23:6

Surely: No "I wonder?" No "I wish!" No "I hope so." Without a doubt. Without a question. Without a concern or worry. Knowing whose I am and who He is. God of His word, God of His promise. God of His covenant. God of His oath. God who cannot and will not fail, falter, or forget.

goodness: Not meanness. Not cruelty. Not unkindness. His goodness. The goodness of God—The goodness in His nature, the goodness in His character, the goodness in His being. Everything about Him good—every thought, every action, every attitude, every decision, every work, every word. Good in His will. Good in His gifts. Good to me. Good every moment. Good all the time. Extending goodness—not as little as He can give, but as much as He can give. Being the best, giving the best, wanting the best. Delighting to shower me with His graciousness—time after time, over and over, now and forevermore.

and mercy: Sweet mercy! Welcomed friend! Wonderful companion! New every morning. Fresh from His heart. Lifting condemnation. Releasing my past. Breaking my chains. Freeing my spirit. Renewing my hope. Securing my future. Mercy upon mercy.

Mine in abundance. Kindly extended. Beautifully given. Graciously bestowed.

shall follow me: Not "There's a good possibility." Not "a 50/50 chance." Will follow! Never to retreat, abandon, or flee. Absolute certainty. Promised by the God who cannot lie. His benefits and blessings—mine to receive. Mine to enjoy. Mine to celebrate. Keeping me from being defeated. Guarding me from being pulled back into my past. Protecting me from being overtaken by things I cannot control. His divine escorts on my pilgrim journey.

all the days of my life: Not once-in-awhile. Not hit-and-miss. Not off-and-on. Not just on good days. Not just on church days. All my days— Cloudy days. Stormy days. Busy days. Quiet days. Days filled with joy. Days filled with sorrow. Days when I feel up. Days when I feel down. Every day. Every moment. Every step. Every breath. Every heartbeat.

and I will dwell in the house of the Lord forever: The forever place—not temporary, not momentary, not transitory. The Father's house. My reserved place. My prepared place. Home! Never to be kicked out, evicted, or left homeless. The place my faith has thought upon. The place my hope is set upon. The place where I belong. The place I was made for. Jesus' place. The place where I am welcomed. The place where I am received. Mine by inheritance. Mine by grace. Mine forever and ever. In the company of the redeemed. In the presence of the Lord. Seeing Him face to face. Knowing even as I am known. Completely fulfilling all my heart has ever longed for since the moment I took my first breath.

Lord,

Thank You for being my Shepherd.

You are good. You are great. You rule over all.
I believe in Your salvation, and I receive
Your forgiveness.

I know that You are good to me
and are doing great things in my life.

Without You I would be a lost sheep,
but because of You, *I am found.*

I trust in You to lead me.
I rely upon You to provide for me.
I look to You as my coming King.
I yield my life and my future to You.

Keep me in Your daily care.

Amen!